VEERE GRENNEY
SEEKING BEAUTY

TO JOHNNY, NATASHA AND CHRISTOPHER

VEERE GRENNEY
SEEKING BEAUTY

PHOTOGRAPHY
FRANCESCO LAGNESE

VENDOME
NEW YORK · LONDON

ON BEAUTY
VEERE GRENNEY
13

THE TEMPLE
SUFFOLK
23

CHESIL COURT
LONDON
80

GAZEBO
TANGIER

HOUSE
109

GARDEN
231

ACKNOWLEDGEMENTS
303

ON BEAUTY
VEERE GRENNEY

I did not have to ask my heart what it wanted
Because of all the desires
I have ever known
Just one thing did I cling to
For it was the essence of all desire
To know beauty

St John of the Cross

At my home Gazebo in Tangier, I have built a wall in the orchard. About a metre wide and three metres high, it sits at the end of a long brick path that is flanked by slender almond trees, persimmon and bergamot, guava, peach, apple and pomegranate. The wall is made from Moroccan tiles and built by local craftsmen, using a technique called *zellige*. Around the edge, The Lord's Prayer is written in Arabic and in the middle, there is a poem by St John of the Cross about the want for beauty. His words speak to me perhaps more profoundly than any others. Here, in the absolute heart of my garden, this poem is an omnipresent reminder that in my lifetime of designing houses I have dreamt beauty, thought beauty and practised beauty. I would like to think that eventually I have become more fluent in beauty and still I'm learning.

When I think back to my early childhood on South Island, New Zealand, I now see that I have always been driven by the fundamental urge to create order and corral objects into some sort of visual harmony. I didn't recognise it as such at the time, but even as a very young child, I couldn't put a cup, a plate, a pencil down on a table without needing to make it look absolutely perfect. That same impulse – the complete desire for beauty - has pervaded every single thing I have done since. It is the force that informs all I do professionally, whether I am designing an apartment in Tel Aviv, a country house in rural England, a beach house in Mustique or a ranch in Wyoming. In my own homes and in the homes of others, I have always looked to create a poetic and deeply pleasing marriage of geometry, comfort, decoration and grace, a marriage that results in a visual accord best described by that one same word, beauty.

Growing up, the thing I loved most was decorating the house with my mother who possessed a finely tuned aesthetic sensibility. I would seriously and meticulously rearrange the living room each time my family moved home, which thankfully, they did quite often. Even then, I instinctively adored houses and was entirely fascinated by every single aspect of them. As a small boy, I remember pedalling my bike round and round the local streets, scrutinising every house in the neighbourhood and really studying them, especially fascinated by places that were mid-construction. At weekends I would cycle over to building sites when no one was around. I was gripped by how people lived in a building, the relationship of the sun to the house and where the light fell. I saw that interior design was about the way we lived; it was absolutely not an exercise in simply shopping, even at its most discerning. It was far more complex, layered and refined than that, about working with the light, the axes of a place. It was about the way you entered a room and the way you left. It was about where you placed furniture. I discovered that the connecting spaces were as important as the big spaces. Entrance halls were crucial and so were passageways. Where did your eye travel when you looked from one room to another? How did you arrive at the view and how did you frame different vistas? At weekends and after school, I avidly devoured all magazines that came my way, finding that these opened up new worlds of avant-garde design, exciting colour combinations and radically different furniture, and introduced me to the authors of these schemes, the interior decorators themselves. In particular, I sought out any English publications that I could get my hands on. And it was here that I first encountered the revolutionary and cosmopolitan David Hicks, a designer who welcomed the modern and the geometric into classical paradigms for a new take on interior decorating. Reading about him as a teenager in 1960's New Zealand, I could never have imagined that I would end up leasing a Palladian fishing lodge in Suffolk that had been restored by Hicks, and that, years later, it would become my own home, The Temple, in the mid 1980's.

By the age of sixteen, I was already–as my sister, artist Sarah Guppy, relates–'a little bit out there' and dedicated to an intense social life that meant going out every single night. At the same time, I knew that the most interesting and compelling thing for me was this nameless art, making beauty in the home. The phrase *interior decoration*, even the concept, did not exist yet in New Zealand. There were no natural routes available or obvious to me, or none that appealed. Possibly I could have made a career working at a haberdashery store, or in a furniture shop called Décor, but that was about it. To pursue what I most loved would mean leaving Auckland and travelling across the world. It took me six more years, a stint at university and a stretch in the Australian outback working in the kitchens of a mobile gas pipeline and driving the trucks when we moved the canteen across the desert. Eventually, I had amassed enough money to set off on the hippy trail. It was 1971 and I was twenty-two. I embarked on a back-to-front version of the usual travellers' route; most hippies at that time were conducting their adventures the other way round, coming from Northern Europe and heading south, down to Australia. But I was determined to get to England on a journey that took me through Nepal, India, Afghanistan and Burma. I

recall it as an extraordinary, hugely influential part of my life, not just the million vivid things I saw in those countries but the encounters with a wildly broad mixture of people – people who, like me, were also seeking novelty, difference and experience. Finally, I arrived in London, the place that was then indisputably the apex of cool.

I was in my early twenties, a long-haired hippy, living in a squat in Little Venice yet simultaneously drawn to a more rarefied world of beauty. It was this compulsion that landed me in the nascent antiques business. At that moment in the 1970's, there was an over-abundance of junk, cheap paraphernalia, real treasures and oddities. You could, and we did, sell just about everything on the Portobello Road in West London. Rents and property were cheap in the area and Notting Hill Gate, Portobello and Ladbroke Grove attracted a whole coterie of burgeoning creatives, artists, photographers, writers, musicians and antique dealers. It was an exciting time, when we were all intrepid seekers or pioneers in our own fields. You could buy and sell furniture and thus express your desire for beauty. Perhaps the biggest revelation that London afforded me was that you could achieve a lifestyle where you actually got paid for doing what you loved–something that surely issued from the most essential part of you. It was a gradual epiphany. For the first time in my life, I saw that this alignment was a real possibility, that there could be a true fusion of what I did and who I was.

After about seven months in England, I was hungry to travel again and I went by boat to Tangier, one of the oldest cities in Morocco. I was particularly attracted to Islamic art and was drawn to Islam itself. As a child, I had always had a strong religious urge and loved places of worship. For a period, I had even planned to go into the church. Much later in my life, the world of spiritual understanding did not come to me from Buddhism, as it did for many of my friends, or from Hinduism; it came to me from the spiritual heart of Islam. I studied the works of the thirteenth-century Sufi prophet, Ibn Arabi. This celebrated Muslim mystic, poet and scholar is widely considered to be the first person to have fully expressed the philosophical and esoteric aspect of Islam. So, while I would always call myself a Christian over all else, I am a Christian with a deep, respectful love for Islam. At that time in my life, my early twenties, I had a yearning for Morocco, a place I had only heard about and imagined. I must have read then that Tangier was a seductive hotbed of aesthetes, eccentrics, alternative mores and

The flat on Jaoquim Nambuco

our view of Copacabana Beach

liberal living. Lying just southwest of Gibraltar, within clear sight of Spain, it is the literal and cultural gateway to Europe. Here, two continents converge, and two oceans –the Atlantic and the Mediterranean–elide. Tangier is a city of many languages (Arabic, Berber, French, English, Spanish) that is predominantly Islamic but friendly to Christianity and Judaism. Famously, it had long exerted a magnetic pull on writers, royalty and artists, free livers and free thinkers. It was home to novelist Paul Bowles and the beat poets William Burroughs, Allen Ginsberg and Jack Kerouac. Tennessee Williams and Matisse spent stints of time here. And Barbara Hutton, the Woolworth heiress, bought a palace in the Casbah after her divorce from Cary Grant. She lived here in the 1940's and hosted wildly flamboyant parties.

No palaces for me, though, when I first arrived. Dishevelled and dungaree-clad, I found myself staying in a cheap hostel. But Tangier somehow worked its reliable magic and I met Mickey Raymond on the beach. He was a decorator for Colefax and Fowler and one of a coterie of British aesthetes who either lived in the city or came there frequently. Mickey took me to a dinner at Villa Léon l'Africain which was hosted by the art historian Richard Timewell. The place was a total revelation, built in 1912 and the most beautiful example of the French colonial style. Timewell had moved here in 1967 after retiring from Sotheby's and brought with him all the possessions of a life dedicated to beauty. Refined and glamorous, the house was surrounded by a magnificent tropical garden, and inside there was a glorious assembly of English furniture, antique fabrics, local finds and objets d'art. I was in love–with that house, with everything about Tangier, the climate, the parties, pleasure, art, hippydom. I loved the Art Deco French buildings. I adored the beach. Everything was here. I travelled further around Morocco, to Essaouira and back, and keenly remember this time in my life as the most wonderful year of meeting people and of freedom.

When I returned to London, I felt I had made a whole world of friends. But I was also penniless and jobless and spent a period sleeping on people's floors until I got a position at Julie's Restaurant, which was at that time the epicentre of Notting Hill. Everyone came there, music business people, movie makers, the Rolling Stones, Princess Margaret, Paul McCartney. At the same time, I managed to lease a shop and start selling furniture.

Suddenly, I possessed a rich social life and a rich creative life, working seven days a week and building the foundations of a career. From there I went on to train under Mary Fox Linton and later I became director of Sibyl Colefax and John Fowler before launching my own company in 1996, Veere Grenney Associates.

There are so many component parts to creating beautiful homes that will transcend the vagaries of fashion. There is real scholarship, years of experience, mistakes made and experiments conducted. There are the accumulated outside influences – the decorators who have gone before me, the greats like Billy Baldwin, Nancy Lancaster, John Fowler, Syrie Maugham, David Hicks. There is practice and more practice and the ineffable thing, something that issues up from the subconscious self, that is an expression of the spiritual, that makes itself manifest in myriad expressions of beauty.

My three homes most eloquently tell the story of who I am, my philosophy, what I have endeavoured to achieve and the lessons that I've absorbed over the years. The Temple is my Palladian folly in rural Suffolk. Chesil Court is my London home, a condensed and cosmopolitan rendering of my favourite design tropes or principles. And then there is the icon, Gazebo in Tangier, which I think is the acme of my creative powers and the culmination of a life's work in the business of understanding, knowing and making beauty. Each place is a summation of forty years spent honing my skills. And each one, I hope, offers up an instance of beauty, an experience of integrity, order and harmony. The Temple in Suffolk is an eighteenth-century fishing lodge, situated deep in Constable's England. Here I have created my own rural arcadia. The pavilion itself is a perfect little Palladian retreat that offers all the bucolic and decorous comforts of an English country house but distilled down to their essence. It sits at the head of a broad artificial canal whose dark waters appear to stretch into the further distance, allowing the mind to travel and inviting contemplation. Inside, I have painted the principal room, the saloon, in my own Temple Pink, a homage of sorts to Nancy Lancaster's legendary hue 'Potted Shrimp'. The furnishings achieve a quality of elegant restraint which allows the original plasterwork, Palladian-style chimney piece and two huge Georgian windows to dominate. These windows offer vistas to the east and west, and remind us that we are at a meeting point of pastoral and arable, cultivated and wild.

Then there is Chesil Court, my apartment in London. Both urban and urbane, this little jewel is the apogee of chic, with its brown cashmere walls in the bedroom, its chrome-yellow kitchen, and its carefully curated collection of pictures. My DNA as an interior designer is here, my greatest influences – in particular, Billy Baldwin – and my favourite motifs, all concentrated into a single space.

Finally, there is my most personal home of all, Gazebo in Tangier, which is to me entirely romantic, seducing you with layer on layer of beauty. I created the house and its Rousseau-esque gardens over the last six years, working from the original 1930's villa and its two acres of long-neglected hillside. Gazebo offers an unparalleled view across a vast expanse of sea and sky towards the tip of Spain and the promise of Europe beyond. There is a poetic symmetry here; Tangier is the city that really opened up the world for me and set me on my path as an interior designer, and it is the city that I have returned to.

Designing these homes and many others, working with inspiring and serious-minded clients, whether with financiers, philanthropists, academics or art-collectors, I have had the opportunity to refine my skills. In creating a starkly glamorous London penthouse, a serene space in the Hamptons, a brilliantly austere contemporary beach house in the Caribbean or the most classical and comfortable grand country home, I have learnt a single enduring truth again and again. It is simply this: beauty does not come from, and cannot come from, a merely educated and cerebral approach to design; that alone is not enough. Beauty comes from a deeper place outside of and beyond logic, which precedes rational thought, the subconscious. And when something stems from the subconscious, it necessarily possesses the profound quality of truth; it is the expression of one's very soul. For me, the aesthetic urge comes necessarily from this spiritual place. It is indisputably the godhead within us all. The business I am in is, at its core, about the manifestation of something in nature which is actually the divine.

But why does beauty even matter? And why do people employ someone to create a beautiful home? Life is, of course, full of perils and struggle, disappointments, loss and muddle. Day-to-day life is consumed with the necessary and the banal. We have a fleeting material existence on this precarious planet. So, what elevates us from the mire? I would argue that beauty unequivocally serves a spiritual purpose. Definitely architecture has always been a spiritual experience for me. There is a geometry in visual harmony that originates in natural forms. We see the Fibonacci sequence repeated in shells, leaves, hurricanes and galaxies. We know that the golden ratio is evident in the work of Palladio, Le Corbusier, Pacioli, Leonardo and Brunelleschi. When you walk into a beautiful space, you respond on some pre-conscious level before the conscious processing of the brain. It is why we may have a powerfully emotional response to visual harmony, certain arrangements of line, shape, colour. I would argue that our own personal encounters with beauty can be tantamount to a transcendental experience, allowing us to briefly transcend the earthly realm. I believe that beauty – in a Keatsian way – allows us access to truth, and that truth, at the heart of all, is really the divine within us. It enables a glimpse of the spiritual other.

My ambition is always to recognise the essence of something, to celebrate that essence and allow it to have its voice. The essence of anything is always perfect, from a flea to a bird, from a bud to a tree. But when it comes to decorating rooms, I endeavour to make some generous refinements and guide everything – views, light, furniture, art, flowers – into harmonious arrangements. The informing principle is geometry. If I do a table-scape, I will spend a long time placing a flower vase perfectly balanced by two candlesticks. It's all about symmetry as a representation of harmony. And then, when the house is done, I hope that these conjunctions of light, colour, shape, pattern and texture, the intimate mix of old and new that I have created, will beckon us into something beyond, the thing that lifts the soul, a beauty that reaches much further that the power of words to convey it.

I think our minds respond to things beyond this world. Take beauty, it's a very mysterious thing is it not?
I think it's a response in our minds to perfection.

Agnes Martin, artist

THE TEMPLE
SUFFOLK

The Temple. What could be more evocative as the name of a house? A temple to classical beauty? To the four seasons? Or to the timeless undulations of the pastoral landscape this Palladian folly occupies in Suffolk, that little patch of England immortalised by John Constable in the early 1800's?

When I reflect on my homes The Temple and Gazebo, the two houses that resonate most profoundly for me, they share essential qualities. Both sit at the apex of east-west vistas and both look out over a long stretch of water that encourages your eye to travel. Beauty and order, romance and comfort, combine in these places that embrace guests and afford me the opportunity to simply be still and read and watch the light.

The Temple has been my heart for the last forty years. It was my salvation, allowing me to escape London and belong to the English countryside. Beyond that, it best expresses my complete journey as a designer, forming a fundamental link between my childhood in New Zealand and my present life here and now. It connects me to one of my earliest influences – David Hicks. I was still at school in Auckland, sixteen years old and passionate about decoration, especially contemporary English interior design. Reading a book about David Hicks, I came across an image of The Temple. When I first saw that picture, I remember thinking there could be nothing lovelier on earth. I stuck it on my study wall as a reminder and possibly a directive.

Many years and many homes later, in 1984, I visited the place as a guest of the renowned antique dealer Charles Beresford Clark. I fell instantly in love with the building. It was, it is, aesthetic perfection, a pavilion sitting theatrically in the most poetic setting. I sold my London flat and took on the lease as soon as it became available. That was 1985 and The Temple remains the house I come to in all seasons for reflection and retreat. When I am here, my life quietens; it is reduced externally (and thus expands internally) to encompass simply this, the house and garden, the local church, the village. It has always been a sacred, comtemplative space for me. Most often I come here on my own, with just my dog Rio by my side, loyal, loving, pale as a ghost. And yet, just as the house and its environs foster calm and contemplation, it is also the perfect place to entertain. Memorably described as 'Palace above and cottage below', The Temple delivers all those glorious, traditional cornerstones of the English country house, the grandest of drawing rooms and most inviting of bedrooms, pristine lawns and pleached limes, a cutting garden dense with dahlias, borders thick with roses and a glasshouse crammed with pelargoniums. And then, woven in, there are little touches of old American glamour, of my New Zealand past: white metal lattice chairs outside the ox-eye window that were originally owned by Bunny Mellon, the 1904 portfolio of ferns from New Zealand hung on the staircase.

David Hicks had discovered the place in 1955, derelict, with flaking stucco, swampy water and just the single dilapidated room. The Temple of the Four Seasons, as it was called then, had once been a fishing lodge, originally built by the architect Robert Taylor around 1750. Taylor had returned to England from his studies in Rome and designed the classical folly to evoke Palladio's summer retreats created for wealthy patrons escaping the heat of Venice. This 'fishing temple' was ideally situated on the estate of Tendring Hall, so that guests staying there could wander down from the big house to fish and stroll along the artificial canal that stretches two hundred yards from the arched loggia of the villa itself. At the heart of the building was a generous saloon of impeccable Palladian proportions, offering aspects east and west. The view to the west was a long slope of farmland, ideal for 'coursing', the ancient English country sport in which greyhounds compete to chase hares. The east view – along the wide canal and then beyond – was more classical, showing, as it still does, a broad stretch of glinting water and the infinite unfolding of the countryside beyond.

When Hicks took on the lease, he restored the roof and dredged the canal. With John Fowler, he planted the two hornbeam hedges that act as 'shoulders' to the house and – with the under-croft – support the central drawing room. What had once been twin dog kennels were transformed into guest bedrooms, and English architect Raymond Erith was employed to put a magnificent ox-eye window into the undercroft. Decorative detail - the fretwork on the banisters leading up to the main bedroom – remains. The house was used for *Vogue* fashion shoots in the 1960s by photographer, Antony Armstrong-Jones, later Lord Snowdon. But Hicks soon moved on and The Temple fell into disrepair and was once again rescued, this time by my friend, Charles Beresford Clark.

The heart of The Temple is the saloon or piano nobile with its twin Georgian windows. This room sits only nine feet off the ground; when you gaze out over the canal, you are tricked into thinking that the water is flowing right under the house. Inside the room, four busts of Roman emperors preside, two at each end, representing the four ages of man. The plasterwork on the ceiling – still in impeccable condition – depicts the four seasons. Here in this flawless Palladian room is all the beauty of Georgian life, the hospitality, communication and regard for aesthetics, like the whole universe in a single cell. Here you are, at the nexus of all.

When I first acquired The Temple, I painted the saloon in Chinese Yellow, a shade that evokes a visceral and joyful response. It was in the mid-1980s and it felt like everyone I worked with wanted a yellow drawing room. In 1995, I changed the walls to flamboyant Kinky Pink then, finally, I altered it once more in 2002 to its current shade, luminous Temple Pink. I was inspired by Nancy Lancaster's legendary Potted Shrimp, one of the greatest ever pinks (not too candy, not too hard, with just a note of brown in it) and I mixed my own hue with her niece Elizabeth Winn. It works beautifully, elegant but not austere, warm but restrained, perennially chic. I deliberately have nothing on the walls in the saloon, so that the architectural details exist as the main story here. The tulipieres atop the mantelpiece are from Christian Dior in the 1950s. Furniture upholstered in my own fabric sits adjacent to nineteenth century antiques. The chandelier is nineteenth century, very simple and a little small; it has been here for thirty years. And I always have giant standard geraniums that fill the alcoves. I have long had a passion for pelargoniums; The Temple has always been full of them, as is my home in Tangier, Gazebo. We always grew them when I was a child in New Zealand, and for me they are the most generous of plants. And in the same spirit of combining the modest with the grand, I have used rush matting on the floors of The Temple, as I have in so many homes that I have designed over the years.

The saloon at The Temple sits at the meeting point of two aspects. To one side lies the rolling arable land of Suffolk; to the other is a canal. The canal had been destroyed by the great storm of 1987, but I restored it with the landlord of the estate and planted twenty-five lime trees along each side. In keeping with the pastoral ideal, I have kept the whole thing very correct: there is no florid or extraneous adornment, no fountain; the canal is simply an unbroken sheet of water that reflects both house and sky and works visually as an avenue. It brokers the transition from the formal house and its topiaried yews and clipped hedges, to the farmland beyond. Traditionally, Palladian villas never had great formal gardens; rather they sat in the countryside itself. In recognition of this, I have kept the more ornamental and colourful parts of the garden hidden. What you can see around The Temple is simply yew and hornbeam, lawn, an ancient oak tree. The prettiness – my rose garden and the dahlia beds, the glasshouse – all this is hidden so that it doesn't interrupt the pastoral ideal. All the vitality and movement come from the light dashing across the water, which itself changes minute by minute. Here on the canal, the ducks come out and everything drops into stillness. I am reminded that everything I need is here, that the whole universe is alive and embodied in the brilliant water of the canal, in this room and in the broader landscape beyond.

RIGHT: *The white, metal lattice chairs outside the ox-eye window were once owned by legendary American gardener and philanthropist, Bunny Mellon, and they add a touch of glamour. I love their eccentric shape abutting the more classically English garden furniture. To each side I grow those staples of an English garden, hollyhocks and white pelargoniums.*

OVERLEAF: *Traditionally, Palladian villas never had great formal gardens. What you can see around The Temple is simply yew and hornbeam, lawn, an ancient oak tree. The rose gardens, dahlia beds and the glasshouse are hidden so that they do not interrupt the pastoral ideal.*

'My life is sustained by the
world of beauty, which you will
see where ever you rest your eyes,
and this beauty is nature itself.'

Khalil Gibran

LEFT & OVERLEAF: *The guest bedrooms – once The Temple's original dog kennels – were converted in the 1950s by David Hicks when he took on the lease. I have designed them to be serene and restrained, using a monochromatic scheme punctuated with the odd note of yellow or pink, and always with fresh flowers from the garden. The wallpaper in the twin bedroom is Tabitha by Veere Grenney for Schumacher. The paintings here are created by or come from friends and family.*

LEFT: *I love rugs on rugs, and here I have placed a Moroccan find on top of the rush matting that I have used throughout the house. Sympathetic, modest and versatile, rush matting will reliably add a quiet warmth and earthy quality to a room.*

OVERLEAF: *David Hicks employed English architect Raymond Erith to put the magnificent ox-eye window into the undercroft, which is now my kitchen and dining room. It contains the view perfectly: you look out onto the lime avenue flanking the broad, artificial canal. The fabric on the screen is Folly by Veere Grenney for Schumacher.*

Looking at the history of my houses, the things that often mean the most to me are not great, nor are they works of art; they are objects that have come from or represent my early home, New Zealand.

Veere Grenney

LEFT: *The ceiling of the saloon displays plasterwork depicting the four seasons. On either side of the large east window are two alcoves that once contained a shepherd and shepherdess, or Adam and Eve. The sweep of the seasons, the span of human life and all of nature is here in microcosm.*

LEFT: *In 2002, I painted the saloon in Temple Pink, a hue inspired by Nancy Lancaster's legendary Potted Shrimp. I mixed this colour with her niece Elizabeth Winn and it works beautifully here. I deliberately have nothing on the walls in the saloon, so that the architectural details exist as the main story. The chandelier is English, possibly eighteenth century, and a little too small so that it does not detract from the view.*

CHESIL COURT
LONDON

The first thing you see when you step into my apartment in Chesil Court, Chelsea, is a terracotta statue on a floating marble shelf in the hallway. Over the years, art, unusual objects and exceptional furniture have come and gone in my life and I find myself increasingly attached to very little. However, there are just a few things that I cannot bear to part with and this is one of them. I bought the statue in the 1970s and suspect it is late nineteenth century English, made in the expressive manner of Lord Leighton. It could be many things, a shrouded Islamic lady, a nun or an Arts and Crafts woman. Both humble and earthy, it is also suggestive of something transcendental and speaks deeply to me. Struck into stillness, it is a quiet reminder of the spiritual influences that inform my own life.

Above the statue is my Craigie Aitchison painting of a Bedlington terrier, crucifix, Holy Island and a boat. In luminous colour the artist conveys poignancy, God, and the impossible mystery of life. His colour, his emotion and his complete integrity all issue from the heart. Here is my spiritual life condensed into a small space. This apartment in Chesil Court epitomizes my life as a designer. It is a distilled essence of my greatest influences, with its strong echoes of Billy Baldwin, David Hicks, and Nancy Lancaster, its notes of Egypt and my favourite art, fabrics and colours.

Chesil Court had been braided into my history, long before I bought this apartment. When I first came to London, I had been initially drawn to Notting Hill and was based there from 1973 to 2003. My office was in Chelsea from the 1980's, but West London was my home. I had an old friend from my childhood in New Zealand, Keith Lichtenstein, who was close to David Hicks and who owned the coolest restaurant in the King's Road, the Casserole. Keith was an avid collector, buying Bacons and Gluck and Mackintosh furniture. He lived in a tiny, glamourous flat in Chelsea, in a block called Chesil Court. Constructed in the late 1930s by the London Power Board, this was a state-of-the art building, the first ever block to have fully heated ceilings, which in turn became heated floors. There are just four lifts that serve two flats on each floor. The building features both Georgian windows and steel – Crittal – windows leading onto the balconies. I particularly love that mix of my two favourite styles, and in the back of my mind I always had the idea that, if I was not living in a house, I would be a resident of Chesil Court. It would be the most perfect pied-à-terre. Then, in 2021, I managed to buy this flat on the sixth floor. It has phenomenal views, looking south to the river in one direction and right over West London in the other. I live in Tangier for most of the year, but when I am in London this place is ideal for my Chelsea office; I can walk to work and back each day. I can be here for the theatre, opera, work and friends. It is like living in the Carlyle Hotel in New York.

The two gifts when I bought the flat were that the building – remarkably – is not listed. The previous owner had knocked all the walls down; so in effect, I was buying a completely open space. These flats are not designed to be big empty studios, so I reinstated three principal rooms, including a sitting room with a balcony that has the most wonderful vista over West London and a bedroom which directly faces Albert Bridge. There would be a perfectly urban kitchen – the antithesis of homely – and the most cosmopolitan of marble bathrooms. Crucially, I created big cupboards. Loving the idea of designing the tiniest, grandest hall in London, I installed inlaid linoleum squares with a star in the middle. Linoleum, which periodically drops in and out of fashion, was the dream

solution here: it is practical, warm to walk on and particularly good for sound insulation. The finished floor is reminiscent of Michael Inchbald's 1960s lino floors which are made to look like marble. The chocolate lacquer walls are something I adore and are a reference – or homage, really – to the legendary decorator Billy Baldwin and his phenomenally chic East Side studio with its high-gloss chocolate walls. However, creating hand-lacquered surfaces is a laborious process. Alistair Erskine, who has worked with me for many years, first beautifully skimmed the walls, then rubbed them with sandpaper over and over again until they were velvet-soft. Lastly, he applied many coats of lacquer. You achieve a greater depth with hand lacquering; it has a beautiful sheen to it but is less reflective. On the adjacent woodwork we created a fine stripe, with a black and brown combing effect. All the doors in the flat are half-glazed with a pleated plain-yellow cotton behind the glass, and the light bounces back and forth between the combed paint, the glossy walls and the glazed door.

I designed the geometric carpet to be a reinterpretation of a David Hicks original. It is used in the sitting room and bedroom and coloured to chime perfectly with the chocolate brown in the hallway, the soft brown cashmere of the bedroom and the chintz on the sitting room walls. Created by Veere Grenney for Schumacher, the chintz is restrained and romantic, in pearl and grey, black and soft fawn. The sofa here is intended to be a little louche. I designed it to be like a Maison Jansen piece in brown silk velvet and it possesses a touch of what I call, Duchess of Windsor style. Above it, hangs a serene abstract painting by Roger Hilton, an artist who is always a touchstone for me. The yellow armchair is essential to the room. Yellow always works in a charming and sophisticated way to add a note of vitality to a space. But perhaps the most important object, and definitely the most personal, is the cerulean-blue vase that once belonged to Cecil Beaton and which has featured in all his homes. I fell in love with it at the 1980 sale held at his home, Reddish House in Broad Chalke, Wiltshire, after he died.

My yellow kitchen feels like a concentrated dose of pure joy. In general, I am not overly fond of kitchens. But this one is empty of any extraneous paraphernalia and is absolutely not domestic. It is painted in the high-gloss chrome yellow that I most love and glazed in white Victorian tiles. Quite simply, it is all light, all pleasure. It faces the courtyard and sitting here for coffee in the morning cannot fail to make you happy.

The geometric carpet continues into my bedroom where it echoes a four-and-a-half-inch windowpane check fabric I designed for Schumacher, which I used for the four-poster bed and the curtains. I covered the walls in a brown cashmere to create a dry repeat of the more liquid shine of the chocolate-brown hallway. In all my schemes, I like the contrast, the friction, that comes from juxtaposing wet and dry, high and low. I put a lacquer finish next to a dry fabric or something completely matt, and I placed the esoteric, the refined or the glamourous adjacent to the plain and the modest. I then decided to hang six ultra-vivid Roger Hilton gouaches on the wall, and one of his charcoals covers the television. Very special to me is the painting by Catalan artist Ramiro Fernández Saus, in which a mouse sits patiently by an artist who is absorbed in the process of making art, recording a palm tree with what could be a pyramid beyond him. These components or apparent themes – the exotic, the Egyptian and the making of art in life – resonate deeply for me.

Finally, I have a gilded crucifix made by my sister, the artist Sarah Guppy, which has always hung by my bed, entirely simple, like a call to integrity. And there it is, complete. Small, super smart, sophisticated and functional, Chesil Court has a place for everything, including my dog. The chintz, the lacquer, the abstract art, the comfort, and the quiet notes of a spiritual life. My apartment is as much a complete expression of me as my other homes. Here in harmony are my loves, my beliefs, my greatest teachers and all I have learnt in this business of beauty.

RIGHT: *I designed the sofa to be like a Maison Jansen piece – sumptuous, grand and faintly louche – in brown silk velvet. Chocolate brown is warm and sophisticated as a shade and works beautifully with yellow, pink, blue – everything, really. It is the colour of the earth and therefore very versatile. The geometric carpet is a reinterpretation of a David Hicks original, the chintz is a Veere Grenney design for Schumacher.*

LEFT & OVERLEAF: *The most important object in the room is my cerulean-blue vase that once belonged to Cecil Beaton. I acquired it when the contents of his final property, Reddish House, went up for auction. Its piercing colour always draws the eye but is never intrusive, and it pairs marvellously with the pops of pink and yellow throughout.*

LEFT & OVERLEAF: *Some of my favourite design motifs come together in the sitting room; a yellow armchair; a classic Thebes stool at an Egyptian-style table, which opens out to become a desk; a grand English chair adding elegance and finesse. The artwork includes paintings by Scottish painter Alan Davie, John Wells, William Scott, Roger Hilton and other post-war St Ives artists. The view across the Thames is incomparable.*

In general, I am not overly keen on kitchens. However, this one is the antithesis of homely. It is painted in the high-gloss vivid colour that I call chrome yellow and glazed in white Victorian tiles. Sitting here for coffee cannot fail to make you happy.

Veere Grenney

RIGHT: *For my bathroom, I have used cloudy-veined marble, bespoke nickel-framed doors and a basin designed especially for the space. The effect is a 1940s glamour that works flawlessly with the sleek, highly detailed and beautifully finished feel of the place.*

LEFT & OVERLEAF: *The geometric carpet continues into my bedroom, where it echoes a four-and-a-half-inch windowpane check fabric I designed for Schumacher. I had planned to line the walls with this cloth, but marrying the squares is difficult unless the room has perfect rectangular surfaces. Instead, I used it for the four-poster bed and the curtains. There is always a pelargonium, as at The Temple and Gazebo. On the bed is a touch of luxury, a sheared mink blanket which I love but which my lurcher loves even more. Roger Hilton gouaches add pops of strong colour. Through the bedroom is my dressing room with its impeccable little Arts and Crafts chair by Godwin.*

GAZEBO
THE HOUSE

Halfway up the Old Mountain in Tangier, my home Gazebo gazes down over a seemingly infinite stretch of brilliant blue, the meeting point of two oceans, the Atlantic and the Mediterranean. The garden that drops towards the sea is a paradise of towering palms, umbrella pines, plumbago, datura, bougainvillea, agapanthus. Terracotta paths are dappled with shade. A serpentine teucrium hedge forms a line of beauty along one of the five terraces and a glasshouse curves round the base of a eucalyptus. There are pools, dark green and milky blue and three springs on the property, one of these providing drinking water said to be sacred. My home here is, for me, the ultimate expression of beauty in the most wonderful location I could ever wish for. Most of all, it is entirely personal. To create this house and garden, I drew on every bit of talent and inspiration I possess; at the age of sixty, I manifested everything I had learnt over the last forty years. Gazebo plaits together all the memories, skills, experience and different influences I have absorbed. In each room there is evidence of a life well travelled, people well met, and beauty assiduously studied. From David Hicks to Syrie Maugham, Felix Harbord to Oliver Messel, Richard Timewell to Christopher Gibbs – they are all here. Then there are the unsung heroes of the place, the Moroccan artisans – carpenters, metalworkers, tilers – who have produced such miraculous work. Gazebo is animated by the people who work here day to day and by my friends and family who come and stay a while.

Tangier has swum in and out of my life since I first arrived as a wild-haired hippy in 1973. It took me twenty years to come back, but I think the exoticism, the light, the play of myriad blues and the innate cosmopolitan quality of the place must have rooted themselves deep in my imagination. Perched at the very top of Africa, looking out to Gibraltar, the whole city is inconceivably romantic. Islamic architecture prevails, punctuated by the odd Art Deco building and then, at the centre, the Anglican church of St Andrew of which– I am a churchwarden. This Moorish building was painted by Matisse in *Landscape Viewed from a Window*. It has the Lord's Prayer written in Arabic around the nave and is emblematic of the history of tolerance here, where Muslims, Christians and Jews have lived together with reciprocal respect. Artists and art lovers, socialites and mavericks, adventurers of all description have long been drawn to the cultural climate in Tangier, coupled with the balmy Mediterranean weather. Mohamed Choukri, Walter Harris, William Burroughs, Truman Capote, Edith Wharton, Tennessee Williams, Gore Vidal, Jean Genet and Gertrude Stein are just a few of those seduced by or belonging to the city.

When I returned to Tangier in the early 1990s, the whole place felt artistic, open and exciting. That first year, the legendary antique dealer Gordon Watson was here, as was journalist Hamish Bowles, and other friends of theirs – polymath artist Patrick Kinmonth, photographer Mario Testino and many others. From then on, I came back faithfully each summer and rented Gordon Watson's house, La Perla. The city was exploding in popularity – new roads, new buildings – but this area, the Old Mountain, still possessed the quality of an eccentric village peopled by aesthetes. Initially, it was my partner David's idea to buy something here, and in 2009 – having sold a property in Rio – I saw this little house that had been built by Hortense Loeb in the 1930s. It had been left to Hortense's daughter Marguerite, a photographer and the wife of celebrated Scottish artist James McBey. Marguerite became a society figure in her own right and eventually, passed the place on to the late Joe McPhillips, a charismatic American who became the headmaster of the American School in Tangier.

When we first looked at it, Gazebo was simply a neglected cottage on a cliff, with two and half acres of jungle around and in front of it – eucalyptus, wattle and laurel, a shaggy tangle of impenetrable undergrowth. The house itself was a modest stucco-clad building, blue with white shutters, a little bit theatrical, with a slightly Caribbean feel. It had not technically come up for sale but was in a complicated legal situation, and my friend Christopher Gibbs, who lived opposite, helped me secure the place. When I bought it, I had no real plan and definitely no grand vision. All I had in mind was a kind of paradigm, the colonial English Regency house. I love colonial buildings, and Regency architecture, particularly that of 1805–1815, is my favourite. There has always been a group of the aesthetically minded who have revered that period. It was evident in the work of British decorator and theatre designer Felix Harbord and that of Oliver Messel costumier, artist and creator of early homes in Mustique and Barbados. It was there in society photographer Cecil Beaton's Reddish House and Ashcombe House.

My initial informing principle was that I knew I had to have an internal courtyard so that when the Sharqi wind came in from the east, there would be a still and sheltered place. And I loved the idea of a colonnade. I had been staying in a magnificent house in Dorset that had a Regency loggia off the drawing room; I took measurements of the arches and columns and we reproduced them to make my colonnade here. But instead of having a solid wall on one side, I created two doors, with a staircase sweeping down into the garden.

As I built new foundations, to shore up the bigger footprint of the house, I came to the idea of staggered terraces, different levels that would each reveal a different vista. In fact, the view from Gazebo is so extraordinary and so huge, that it felt crucial to encounter it in stages and increments through the house. To achieve this, I grew a hedge around the entrance courtyard, so that when you initially come in, you are not even aware of the view. Then you step into the elliptical entrance hall, a serene and softly glowing space that has a hallowed feeling and creates a moment of pause. Completely unadorned except for a scarlet ibis and flowers, the only detail here comes from the golf ball cornicing and the smudgy cream and tan striations in the travertine flooring. This oval hallway is based on an original John Soane design and is a beautiful oval egg shape, always more interesting than a rectangle or a square. And in this instance, the hallway was a means to disrupt the central sightline that runs from the one end of the house to another.

As you progress into the colonnade, you come upon a tantalising glimpse of the garden. There's a seduction in this gradual reveal, it is subtle and more beguiling than instant spectacle. You are immersed in a full sensory experience, the scent of gardenias and the orange trees. Everywhere there are ferns, jasmine, lilies and pelargoniums. There is the sound of water, gentle and incessant, from the fountain in the courtyard.

Elegant and formal, the drawing room is both architecturally refined and highly decorative. I created the curved walls, the columns and the vaulted Soane-esque ceiling to render it perfectly classical. The Soane ceiling is possibly a bit of madness but I love it, and the ovals and curves repeat in hedging the garden. The upholstered walls are hung with pictures that all share a quality of foreignness: either they issue from some other place or depict a foreign land. There is a Tangier seascape by Sir John Lavery from 1910, paintings by James McBey and a luminous picture of Tangier in 1680 by an artist called Van Hoek. It was sold to me by Christopher Gibbs because he wanted it to remain in Tangier, its natural home.

For utter charm, I adore my mauve-grey dining room, evoking Syrie Maugham with its plaster palm-tree pilasters. Here I have created what I call the Great Wall of China, tiers of circa 1815 Royal Worcester plates from a 250-piece chinoiserie service I found in Paris; I decided to build a plate cupboard where the plates are exposed. The blue-rimmed set of china once belonged to Nancy Lancaster, the gold was a lucky find at auction. Beyond the dining room is the library, one of my favourite rooms. Here there are more wonderful pictures: another James McBey, an Oliver Messel painting of Barbados and Roger Fry's allegorical portrait of Florence. Bugatti inlaid furniture adds a Moorish quality that marries with the walls. In winter, I have a fire burning in here day and night, a welcome retreat as the temperature falls.

All art is an attempt to
manifest the face of God in life

Cecil Collins

LEFT: *Gazebo sits at the top of the Old Mountain in Tangier, and it was the impossibly generous view and the two and a half acres on a cliff that immediately tugged at my heart strings. The vista simply takes your breath away. Practically and intuitvely it became clear that terraces would be key, the most elegant and sympathetic solution to my garden-on-a-cliff. I turned to the hugely talented Christopher Masson to plant the different levels which would allow distinct zones of beauty, places to be and spaces to pause and absorb the view; they would enable a staggered descent both really and visually.*

A scarlet ibis
adds a note of vivid colour
and evokes ancient Egypt,
where the bird was
considered sacred.

Veere Grenney

RIGHT: *The Moroccan brickwork used here and in the garden is bejmat. It feels soft to walk on and is many shades of terracotta. Andalucian green and white olive bowls hang on the cloister wall, which is painted pinky brown. The rugs are Moroccan and the striped fabric is Rafe, a Veere Grenney design for Schumacher. Nancy, my Moroccan rescue dog, is always a crucial part of the tableau, and is highly aware of the perfect contrast between her bronze coat and the scarlet rug beneath her.*

LEFT: *I always have incense burning in the treillage room. Flowers fill the table in the middle of the space, which is panelled with intricate treillage and marries Colefax rose chintz curtains, rattan chairs, a local lantern and a square skylight. All this is anchored on one of the Mauritanian straw and leather rugs that I use throughout the house.*

Beauty and happiness and life
are all the same thing and they are
pervasive, unattached and abstract
and they are our only concern.
They are immeasurable.

Agnes Martin

RIGHT: *In the drawing room, the curved walls, columns, vaulted Soane-esque ceiling and golf ball cornicing create a classical effect. The upholstered walls are hung with pictures that share a quality of foreignness. There is a 1910 Tangier seascape by Sir John Lavery, but the larger picture here is a depiction of Tangier in 1680 by an artist called Van Hoek. It was sold to me by Christopher Gibbs because he wanted it to stay in Tangier.*

OVERLEAF: *Another view of the drawing room shows a 1930s chandelier by Maison Jansen. The chairs are from a set of fifty made in 1790 and come from an Austro-Hungarian palace. The rush matting is a Veere Grenney design, created to be thin and slightly 1930s looking.*

141

RIGHT: *The library is a perfect rectangle that delivers those twin necessities, a view and a fireplace. I wanted it hand-painted in a Moroccan Orientalist way and employed Alistair Erskine, the trompe l'oeil decorative painter, to move in for three months and create panels of faux tilework in echo of Renzo Mongiardino.*

OVERLEAF: *More of my favourite pictures hang in the library, another James McBey, an Oliver Messel painting of Barbados and Roger Fry's allegorical portrait of Florence. Bugatti inlaid furniture adds a Moorish quality that marries with the walls. In the winter, I have a fire burning day and night.*

LEFT: *I propagate cuttings and grow plants from seed year-round in the polytunnel and cultivate carnations and pelargoniums in the curved glasshouse in shades of fuchsia, palest pink, magenta and blood red. Pelargoniums link me to my childhood and to my home in Suffolk, The Temple, where they are placed all around the house. Initially I had planned to make the greenhouse a spot for outdoor dining. But although I abandoned that first notion, I hung onto the circular shape, and built this glass semi circle, complete with a little sink and curved bench.*

RIGHT: *Christopher Masson helped me arrange the garden into distinct areas. We used clipped evergreen and teucrium domes and hedges to form a framework and then created the English herbaceous border, the exotic garden, the succulent garden and the tropical zones. All these coalesce around the central pond on the Long Walk, which travels from one end of the garden to the other. Twelve olive trees flank this path, offset by an undulating teucrium hedge below, that forms a classic line of beauty. Below the orchard – planted with grapefruit, bergamot, lime, kumquat, persimmon, guava, quince, peach and almond – is the second gazebo, a pale, ornate roof rising out of the trees. It serves to contain the view; a last note of the decorative and the formal.*

LEFT: *On the property are three natural springs, one of which is said to be sacred. A domed building over one of these draws your eye from the swimming pool and echoes the dome of the pool house, which appears to almost float amidst the palms. A slender rill flows into the ponds below. The greater part of the planting here is wildly verdant tropicana, papyrus, elephant ears, strelitzias, tractor seat plants and ginger. The paths are softest pink terracotta bejmat clay bricks, found locally and installed by local craftsmen.*

ACKNOWLEDGEMENTS

Over my life, I have had the immense good fortune to live in many lovely homes, some modest and some less so. I have been blessed with the ability to – whether consciously or subconsciously – marry comfort with form. My three homes that appear in this book are, I hope, apt demonstrations of this.

Architecturally, The Temple is a place of great beauty and I am fortunate to have been its custodian for the last thirty-eight years. After the great storm of 1987, I was lucky to be able to restore the canal and avenue of limes with my late landlord, Sir Joshua Rowley. My thanks to all the individuals who, over the years, have enhanced and continue to enhance, The Temple.

The evolution of Gazebo continues to be a collective achievement. Architect Cosimo Sesti and garden designer Christopher Masson were fundamental in the creation of the garden. My wonderful team there are led by Mouhcin, my house manager. His attention to detail enables the magic of the place to really happen. Tangier has brought with it a cherished collection of friends and my valuable connection with St Andrew's Church.

I would like to thank Vendome Press who have made this project possible, particularly Beatrice and Roger. Photographer Francesco Lagnese and stylist Carolyn Englefield have been a dream team, as evidenced by the beautiful images here.

I also want to thank all the people at my office. In particular, Natasha Greig, Lavinia Younger and the architectural team, led by Bob Walker, who is now ably supported by Daisy Klyhn.

My urban life for the last forty years has been beautifully taken care of by my housekeeper Theresa. Now that she is sensibly retiring, her friend Fatima will take over the task.

Finally, I am eternally grateful to have an incredibly supportive and loving family – my parents, brother, sisters and my beloved nieces and nephews.

First published in 2024 by The Vendome Press
Vendome is a registered trademark of The Vendome Press, LLC
www.vendomepress.com

PALM BEACH
P.O. Box 566
Palm Beach
FL 33480

LONDON
Worlds End Studios,
132-134 Lots Road,
London, SW10 0RJ

PUBLISHERS
Beatrice Vincenzini, Mark Magowan & Francesco Venturi

COPYRIGHT
© 2024 The Vendome Press, LLC

TEXT
Copyright © 2024 Tree Sherriff

PHOTOGRAPHY
Copyright © 2024 Francesco Lagnese

ADDITIONAL IMAGES
Page 168, © 2024 Simon Upton
Page 302, © 2024 Lawrence Mynott

All rights reserved. No part of the contents of this book may be reproduced in whole or in part without prior written permission from the publishers

Distributed in North America by Abrams Books. Distributed in the UK, and rest of the world, by Thames & Hudson
ISBN: 978-0-86565-433-4

EDITOR Catharine Snow
PRODUCTION MANAGER Amanda Mackie
PRODUCTION DIRECTOR Jim Spivey
DESIGN & ART DIRECTOR Roger Barnard

Library of Congress Cataloging-in-Publication Data available upon request

Printed and bound in China by 1010 Printing International Limited
SECOND PRINTING